NEW TECHNOLOGY

military technology

Ian Graham

Evans

Published by Evans Brothers Limited

© 2008 Evans Brothers Ltd

Evans Brothers Limited
2A Portman Mansions
Chiltern Street
London W1U 6NR

First published 2008

British Library Cataloguing
in Publication Data
Graham, Ian 1962-
    Military technology. - (New technology)
    1. Military art and science - Technological
    innovations - Juvenile Literature
    I. Title
    623

    ISBN 978 0 23753 428 8

Printed in China

Credits

Series Editor: Paul Humphrey
Editor: Gianna Williams
Designer: Keith Williams
Production: Jenny Mulvanny
Picture researchers: Rachel Tisdale
    and Laura Embriaco
Consultant: Iain MacGregor, author and
editor specialised in military history.

Acknowledgements

Title page: Northrop Grumman Integrated
Systems; p.6 Msgt Thomas J. Menequin,
USAF/Department of Defense; p.7 U.S. Air
Force; p.9 Dennis Rogers/U.S. Air Force;
p.10 Department of Defense; p.11 David
Gossett, Teledyne Ryan Aeronautical/
Department of Defense; p.12 Northrop
Grumman Integrated Systems; p.13 Boeing;
p.14 R. D. Ward, CIV/Department of
Defense; p.15 Berkeley Robotics and Human
Engineering Laboratory; p.16 ©2007 Vecna
Technologies, Inc.; p.17 Mass Communication
Specialist 3rd Class Kenneth G. Takada/U.S.
Navy; p.18 Master Sgt. Ken Hammond/
Department of Defense; p.19 LCPL Sarah M.
Harman, USMC/Department of Defense;
p.20 Naval Sea Systems Command/U.S.
Navy; p.21 Kockums AB; p.22 General
Dynamics/U.S. Navy; p.24 YN1 Ivan Rivera,
USN/Department of Defense; p.25 top
Photographer's Mate 2nd Class Lynn
Friant/U.S. Navy; p.25 Wikimedia
Commons; p.26 Tech. Sgt. Shane A.
Cuomo/U.S. Air Force; p.27 Tech. Sgt. Paul
Dean/U.S. Air Force; p.28 R. Fearing/UC
Berkeley; p.29 Lockheed Martin; p.31
Eamonn Bourke, Army.mil; p.32 Randy
Montoya/Sandia National Laboratories; p.33
Airman 1st Class Gina Chiaverotti/Army.mil;
pp.34-35 Courtesy of Taser International;
p.37 American Technology Corporation;
p.38 Reynolds/Department of Defense; p.39
U.S. Department of Defense; p.40 U.S.
Department of Defense/ Science Photo
Library; p.41 Michael Savell/Department of
Defense; p.42 Ed Kashi/Corbis; p.43 Peter
Macdiarmid/Getty Images.

This book was prepared for Evans Brothers
Ltd by Discovery Books Ltd.

contents

introduction

Military technology is enormously varied. It includes land, sea and air vehicles of all sorts, communications and computer systems, weapons, satellites and robots. This technology is constantly being updated as military forces try to stay one step ahead of each other.

How is new military technology developed? Military technology cannot stand still. Each time a new development provides a better means of attack, it has to be answered by a better means of defence. The best guns, tanks, fighter-planes, warships and missiles give one side an advantage in battle... until someone else develops even better versions of the same. Military scientists and engineers are constantly looking for new ways of using materials, engines and electronics to improve on existing technology. Sometimes, military forces spot a need for a particular system, vehicle or weapon, perhaps a new type of plane or warship. The government may ask manufacturers to come up with designs. Two or more of the ideas put forward may then be built and tested to find the best.

Monitoring communications during a military exercise. Better, faster communications technology is crucial to military success.

Not all new designs go on to be adopted by the armed forces. The US Air Force decided not to develop the Northrop YF-23 prototype fighter (above).

The successful design will go on to be manufactured and issued to military forces.

Reaching further The range, or reach, of weapons has increased greatly. The first weapons made thousands of years ago were used in hand-to-hand fighting or as far away as someone could throw them. Modern artillery can fire exploding shells more than 30 km and the most powerful rocket-propelled missiles can travel 8,000 km.

What does it cost? As military technology has advanced, its cost has soared. A modern fighter plane costs about £150 million to develop and build. A modern bomber plane costs more than £1 billion. A Nimitz class nuclear-powered aircraft carrier costs about £2.2 billion.

Some countries spend a lot more money on military technology than others. The USA spends the most by a long way. Its military spending is nearly 10 times more than the next biggest spender, China. In fact, the USA spends more than the next 14 countries added together.

This book reveals the latest military equipment in service today and looks at the new military technology that is coming in the next few years.

CHAPTER 1
military aviation

Aviation is one of the most competitive areas of military technology. The leading military powers keep trying to outdo each other in the design of better, faster and more manoeuvrable combat planes.

Why are fighters so important?

Military action often begins with an attack from the air to clear the sky of enemy aircraft and destroy enemy tanks, radar, missile launchers and other threats on the ground. Winning the air war enables ground forces to move in more easily. This is the job of the fighter.

Stealth planes

A whole new generation of fighter planes is entering service. The first of these is the F-22 Raptor, made by Lockheed Martin and

A stealth plane's shape reflects radar waves away from the dish that sent them.

Boeing. Its engines are more advanced, its electronic systems are smarter and it is a stealth plane. The B-2 Spirit bomber is a stealth plane too. It served in the Kosovo War, the invasion of Afghanistan and both Gulf wars.

HOW IT WORKS

A stealth plane is designed to be almost invisible to radar. Its shape reflects radar waves away from enemy radar instead of towards it. The plane can also be covered with special materials that soak up some of the radar waves instead of reflecting them.

Signal is reflected away from ground station

Radar signal from ground station

An Osprey tiltrotor hovers in the air. Its spinning rotors provide all the lift needed to support its weight. They enable it to take off and land without a runway.

Vertical take-off Military forces use a variety of vertical take-off aircraft. Nearly all of them are helicopters. There are small attack helicopters like the US Apache and German Tiger, bigger medium-lift helicopters like the Black Hawk and even bigger heavy-lift transport helicopters like the twin-rotor Chinook. Now there is a new type of vertical take-off aircraft called a tiltrotor. It has rotors like a helicopter and wings like a plane. To take off, its propellers work like helicopter rotors. They lift it straight up in the air. After take-off, its engines and propellers tilt forwards and it flies like a normal plane.

A fighter of the future – the F-35

The F-35 Lightning II is a future fighter being developed now. The US Air Force, US Navy and US Marines will all fly the F-35. These three military services need different types of aircraft, so three different F-35s will be built. The F-35 flown by the Marines, for example, will be able to land vertically. The F-35 flown by the Navy will be designed specially for use on aircraft carrier ships. More than three-quarters of their parts will be the same, so building the planes and repairing them will be easier, faster and less expensive. Like the F-22, the F-35 will be a

WHAT'S NEXT?

Hypersonic combat planes are planes that can fly faster than five times the speed of sound. Hypersonic planes could fly to anywhere in the world within a couple of hours. The US Air Force plans to have a manned hypersonic fighter flying by about 2025.

Planes without pilots It is possible for a pilot to fly a plane without actually being in the plane! The plane is flown by remote control from the ground. Planes like this are called UAVs (Unmanned Air Vehicles) or RPVs (Remotely Piloted Vehicles). These planes are mainly used to gather information about the enemy. The 15-metre long Predator spy-plane is a UAV. Predator has been in service with the US Air Force since 1995. It has been used in the Balkans, Afghanistan, Yemen and Iraq. It has also been used by the Italian Air Force since 2004 and the RAF since 2006.

stealth plane. The first F-35s should begin entering service in about 2011. In addition to the US military, the British Royal Air Force and Royal Navy, as well as the Italian Navy, will also fly them.

The most advanced UAVs do not even need a pilot on the ground. They are programmed with a mission

The Lockheed Martin F-35 Lightning II future fighter is being developed from its X-35 experimental aircraft. The F-35 is expected to cost US $40 billion to develop.

The Global Hawk unmanned spy-plane can survey, in one day, an area equivalent to the country of Greece.

HOW IT WORKS

The pilot of an unmanned air vehicle sits in a cockpit on the ground. The pilot looks at screens showing live images from cameras in the plane. When the pilot moves the controls, radio signals are sent to the plane to steer it.

and then they fly from take-off to landing under the control of their own computers.

Unmanned fighters The next generation of unmanned military aircraft will be fighters. Unmanned fighters are called UCAVs (Unmanned Combat Air Vehicles). They are already being built and flight-tested

FOR AND AGAINST

For

- UCAVs are smaller and more manoeuvrable than manned fighters.
- They can go into action without risking the lives of pilots.
- They can deal with the most heavily defended targets in the early days of a war, to make the sky safer for the manned fighters that will follow them.

Against

- As pilots are not in danger, there may be a greater temptation to go to war.
- If a UCAV developed a fault, it could attack friendly forces or civilians by mistake.

by manufacturers in France and the USA. UCAVS are faster and more manoeuvrable than UAVs. They are expected to start service some time after 2010.

Laser planes A laser is a device that produces an intense beam of pure light. Lasers are used in DVD players and communications. There are military lasers too, but until now they have been used mostly in weapons-guidance systems, not as weapons.

Below is a computer-generated image of a UCAV destroying a target. This UCAV is being developed by the Joint Unmanned Combat Air Systems (J-UCAS) project. Experimental planes have already been built and flown.

HOW IT WORKS

When a high-power laser is fired from an aircraft, it produces intense heat in the target. This weakens the target or even cuts through it. It could make a plane or a missile break up in the air or make its fuel explode.

The ABL airborne laser missile system aims a laser at its target from the nose of the aircraft, which can rotate.

A laser gun-sight sends out a thin beam of light for aiming a gun. Tank gunners use laser range-finders to measure the distance to a target. Lasers are also used in devices called target designators. They fire a laser beam at a target such as a building. A laser-guided bomb steers itself towards the laser reflection and hits the target. Now, super-powerful lasers are being developed as weapons for military aircraft. The aircraft company Boeing will soon begin tests of laser planes.

WHAT'S NEXT?

An aircraft laser being developed now is so powerful that it will be able to destroy a target 15 kilometres away. The planes that will have this laser, the Boeing 747 freighter and the C-130 Hercules aircraft, have already made test flights and the high-power laser weapon has been tested on the ground.

CHAPTER 2
land warfare

Land warfare depends on soldiers, and soldiers depend on their weapons, vehicles, protective clothing and equipment. In the next 20 years, these will be transformed, making future soldiers better protected, better armed, better informed and more comfortable.

Military clothing In the past, a uniform simply identified a soldier's fighting force and rank. Today, the high-tech materials combat clothing is made from protect soldiers from all sorts of weather. There is also special-purpose clothing made of materials that give extra protection from fire or from nuclear, biological or chemical attacks. New military clothing in development does a lot more than this. Borrowing a system already used in spacesuits, a new layer next to the skin will have liquid circulating through it to keep the soldier at a comfortable temperature, however hot or cold the weather. The uniform may also have sensors embedded in it to monitor the soldier's heart rate, temperature and other factors. Problems with the soldier's health

The US Army's prototype combat uniform is presented at a press briefing at the Pentagon, the headquarters of the US Department of Defense. The helmet is fitted with video cameras and satellite navigation. The uniform is armoured and can be heated or cooled.

will be relayed to commanders and if a soldier is wounded, the system will give vital information to medics.

Armoured uniforms As well as a helmet, soldiers can wear a flak jacket designed to stop bullets and flying debris from explosions. They often wear body armour too for extra protection. This is made of hard plates that fit inside pockets in a special vest. Future soldiers will wear clothing that stays flexible until a bullet hits it, when it instantly hardens like armour plate. It sounds like science fiction, but it already exists and two different versions have been developed by companies in the United States. It is based on new materials made of super-strong fibres that lock together only when they are hit hard.

Military robots Robot vehicles already help with bomb disposal and reconnaissance. Some are small enough and light enough to be carried on a soldier's back. The loads they can carry include cameras and mechanical pincers.

Some of the remote-control robots in use today have already been fitted

This soldier is wearing a prototype 'lower extremity exoskeleton'. The powered leg braces enable a soldier to carry heavy loads more easily. The exoskeleton supports the weight of the backpack.

WHAT'S NEXT?

Future soldiers will be able to wear robot-like limbs called exoskeletons. An exoskeleton enables a soldier to move faster or carry heavier loads. One exoskeleton already tested enabled soldiers to lift a 110 kg load as if it weighed only 4.5 kg. Another one enabled its wearer to move twice as fast as normal.

A Battlefield Extraction-Assist Robot (BEAR) demonstrates how it can pick up a wounded soldier. When it finds a casualty, it slides its arms underneath.

with guns. A camera on the robot lets a soldier aim and fire the weapon from up to one kilometre away. These armed robots are about to go into military service. Armed robot sentries have also been developed for guarding a country's borders.

One of the most dangerous jobs during a battle is the rescue of wounded soldiers. A robot called BEAR (the Battlefield Extraction-Assist Robot) has been designed to find and rescue wounded soldiers. A prototype has already been built.

Military vehicles Military vehicles range from small transport vehicles like the versatile Hummer to bigger and more powerful armoured fighting

vehicles. The most heavily armoured military vehicles are tanks. Tank armour used to be made of thick metal, but modern tank armour is made of top secret multi-layered plates of metal, ceramic and plastic. Some tank armour is even designed to explode when a

WHAT'S NEXT?

Military planners think robots will become increasingly human-like and able to act on their own. They will have enough artificial intelligence to find their own way around, identify enemy forces and decide what to do.

A Talon military robot searches for a terrorist bomb, while a small spy-craft called a Micro Air Vehicle (MAV) hovers overhead. Pictures from the MAV are used to guide the robot to the most promising areas.

Nuclear weapons Weapons of all sorts are used in warfare, from pistols and rifles for close combat to mortars and tanks for short-range action, and artillery for long-range attack. There are also missiles ranging from small short-range weapons fired from a soldier's shoulder to long-range missiles that can span an ocean.

Nuclear weapons are the most powerful of all. They are also known as weapons of mass destruction (WMD), because they can kill very large numbers

missile hits it, to stop the missile from bursting through it. Tanks can weigh up to 70 tonnes. The tracks around their wheels spread their weight over a large area and stop them from getting bogged down in soft ground.

HOW IT WORKS

There are two main types of nuclear weapon – the atom bomb and the hydrogen bomb. An atom bomb works by breaking big atoms of uranium or plutonium apart. Each time an atom splits, it gives out a burst of energy. Millions of these add together to make a huge explosion. A hydrogen bomb produces an even more powerful explosion by slamming very light atoms together.

of people. One nuclear weapon may be as powerful as several million tonnes of ordinary explosives. There have been many tests of nuclear weapons, but only two have ever been used in war. They were the atom bombs dropped on the Japanese cities of Hiroshima and Nagasaki at the end of World War II.

Nuclear proliferation Since the first nuclear weapons were developed, a growing number of countries have acquired them. As each country 'goes nuclear', its possible enemies race to produce their own nuclear weapons. In time, most developed countries may have nuclear weapons. This may not make a full-scale nuclear war more likely, because any country that carries out a nuclear attack on another nuclear state knows that it risks suffering a devastating nuclear counter-attack. This is called Mutually Assured Destruction, or MAD. It has

prevented nuclear war until now. However, as the number of nuclear-armed states grows, there is more chance of a nuclear weapon being used by accident or falling into the hands of terrorists.

WHAT'S NEXT?

Small nuclear artillery shells and bombs could be used in future as 'bunker-busters' to destroy heavily strengthened underground buildings. A bunker-buster is designed to penetrate earth, rock or concrete before its warhead explodes, instead of exploding in the air or on the surface. They have a very strong casing that can survive smashing into the ground. One version of the American B-61 nuclear bomb is a nuclear bunker-buster. It is designed to detonate 1.2 metres underground and produce a shock wave powerful enough to crush a bunker below it.

The B-61 nuclear bomb is designed to be dropped by US and NATO warplanes. There are different versions of the bomb with different yields (explosive power). It can be as powerful as a few hundred tonnes, or up to a maximum of 340,000 tonnes of normal explosives.

Dirty bombs A nuclear weapon doesn't have to produce a nuclear explosion to be effective. Simpler weapons called 'dirty bombs' spread radioactive material over a wide area instead of producing a nuclear blast. A dirty bomb could make a modern city uninhabitable for decades. Dirty bombs have already been used. A dirty bomb was planted in Moscow by Chechen rebels in 1995, but it didn't explode. It was found and defused. Along with dynamite, it contained radioactive Caesium-137 taken from cancer treatment equipment. In London in 2006, Dhiren Barot was convicted of planning dirty bomb attacks in the UK and USA.

Military staff check for radioactive contamination from a simulated dirty bomb attack during an exercise. Their suits protect them from radioactive particles falling on their skin or being breathed in.

FOR AND AGAINST

For
- Nuclear weapons deter countries from attacking a nuclear state, because they risk a nuclear counter-attack.

Against
- Nuclear weapons are incredibly expensive.
- As more countries acquire them, there is a greater risk of a nuclear accident.
- They are useless against terrorist organisations.
- They are indiscriminate. They can kill hundreds of thousands of people at a time.
- The radioactive fall-out from a nuclear explosion damages the environment and people's health for decades and over a wide area.

CHAPTER 3
warships and submarines

Nations have used warships to spread their power overseas and control sea routes for centuries. Modern warships are big, slow targets that are very easy to find and attack. Future warships will be faster and harder to find. Under the waves, faster submarines armed with faster weapons are being developed too.

Sea giants The biggest and most powerful warships ever built are the US Navy's Nimitz-class aircraft carriers. Each of these giant ships is 317 metres long, weighs 100,000 tonnes and carries up to 90 aircraft. The ship and its aircraft need a total crew of nearly 6,000. Nuclear-powered engines give it a top speed of more than 55 kph. Nimitz-class carriers served as floating military airports during both Gulf wars.

Stealth warships An enemy cannot attack a ship it cannot find. Warships are normally found by radar, so they need to have a shape that makes it hard for radar to spot them, just like stealth planes. The shape of a stealth warship stops enemy radar waves from being reflected back where they came from, so the ship disappears from radar screens.

The US Navy's Sea Shadow *stealth warship was the first stealth warship to be designed. It floats on two hulls, hidden under the water.*

The US Navy experimented with a stealth ship called *Sea Shadow* in the 1980s. The first stealth ship to enter service with a navy was the Swedish Navy's *Visby*, launched in 2000. *Visby* is also the biggest ship to be built from carbon fibre, a super-strong plastic material used to make racing cars. Norway, France, Germany, Britain, India and Singapore have stealth warships too. The US Navy's next stealth ship is the DD(X). It produces an echo, or blip, on a radar screen 50 times smaller than other warships. The first DD(X) ship, the USS *Zumwalt*, is due to enter service in about 2013.

The Swedish Navy's Visby *is a stealth ship. Its sloping sides reflect radio waves away from their source. This and a plastic hull make the ship almost undetectable by radar.*

Naval guns In the past, battleships were armed with mighty guns. A World War II battleship could hurl a shell weighing 1,225 kg a distance of more than 32 km. Modern warships are armed with missiles. A Harpoon ship-to-ship missile has a range of 140 km. Future warships may be armed with guns once more, but they will be a completely new type of gun called a railgun. A railgun fires a projectile so fast that it can reach the horizon

The Littoral Combat Ship (LCS) is a new warship being developed for the US Navy. It is a high-speed trimaran (three hulls) designed to operate in shallow coastal waters. A flight deck at the back serves as a landing platform for helicopters.

WHAT'S NEXT?

Some future warships may have three hulls instead of one. Ships with three hulls are called trimarans. Trimaran racing yachts and powerboats are common, but now trimarans are being designed as warships. They are very stable and fast, and they can operate in rough seas.

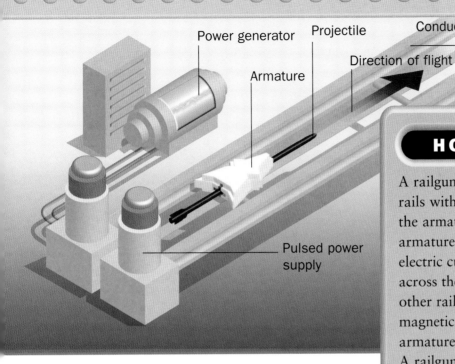

Power generator   Projectile   Conducting rails

Armature   Direction of flight

Pulsed power supply

A railgun uses a massive electric current to launch a projectile from between a pair of rails.

in only six seconds. It can also fire a projectile so high that it goes into space, and then uses satellite navigation to aim itself at a target before it falls back to Earth. Experimental railguns have already been built in the UK and the United States. The first railgun-armed warship could be in service by 2020.

Submarines All the major military powers have submarines. They dive by letting seawater flood into tanks inside them, so that they become heavier than the surrounding water. Modern submarines can dive to a depth of 240-300 metres. At this depth, the sea squeezes a submarine's hull

HOW IT WORKS

A railgun has two parallel conducting rails with a block of metal, called the armature, between them. The armature slides along the rails. A huge electric current is sent down one rail, across the armature and back up the other rail. This produces a powerful magnetic field, which makes the armature accelerate down the rails. A railgun projectile is a lump of metal, like a rifle bullet, only bigger. It's not like an artillery shell or guided missile – it has no explosives inside it. It travels so fast that it hits its target with as much energy as a conventional exploding shell. The projectile sits on the front of the armature, or inside it, and is shot from the end of the rails.

A railgun does not need the explosive charges that usually launch shells from guns. The projectile itself does not even need an explosive warhead. It hits a target so fast that it does not need to explode to destroy it. So, warships armed with railguns do not need to carry lots of highly explosive shells and charges. A naval railgun could replace the 'million-dollars-a-shot' missiles that are used today, at a fraction of the cost.

Naval officers man their battle stations onboard the US Navy submarine Charlotte. *The USS* Charlotte *is a nuclear-powered attack submarine.*

WHAT'S NEXT?

Some people think it might be possible to build a supersonic submarine! The US Navy tested a supersonic underwater weapon in 1997, so it is certainly possible for something to travel at supersonic speeds underwater.

25-30 times more powerfully than at the surface. If it dives too deep, water pressure will crush it.

There are different types of submarines. Attack submarines hunt enemy submarines and surface ships and attack them. Bigger ballistic missile submarines patrol the oceans, staying hidden deep underwater. Their nuclear-powered engines enable them to stay underwater for several months. They make their own water and oxygen. The only reason they have to come to the surface is to fill their food stores. They carry a deadly cargo of nuclear weapons. They do not attack other vessels. In fact, they avoid all other shipping. Their job is to deter anyone from making a nuclear attack on their country. If this were to happen, these submarines could unleash a terrible counter-attack.

The USS Florida *powers through the water. The* Florida *is one of the US Navy's nuclear-powered Ohio-class guided missile submarines.* Florida *is armed with cruise missiles.*

Underwater rockets The torpedo is the submarine's standard weapon. Once launched into the water, it homes in on the sound of its target. When a vessel is attacked by torpedoes, its crew has a short time to take defensive action. A faster underwater weapon would give the target no time to react. Russia has developed just such a weapon, an underwater missile called Shkval. It is about four times faster than a normal torpedo.

HOW IT WORKS

The Shkval is fired from a submarine's torpedo tube. It has a rocket which propels it through the water at 360 kph. It travels inside a coating of air bubbles that stream out of its nose. The bubbles stop the surrounding water from slowing it down.

A close-up of the Shkval underwater rocket shows clearly the hole at the tip of its nose where air streams out.

An artist's impression of what Lockheed's high-altitude airship will look like.

WHAT'S NEXT?

Unmanned high-altitude airships will be able to circle over a trouble-spot for days or weeks, relaying pictures by satellite to their base. These airships are filled with helium, a gas which is lighter than air. Lockheed is developing a high-altitude airship that will monitor a 1,000-km wide area of the ground from 20 kilometres up. It will be nearly 152 metres long and up to 45 metres in diameter.

the Navy may want to board and search. Soldiers can also use them to check out an area before they advance into it. A soldier launches an MAV by starting its engine and throwing it into the air. The operator then steers the plane to the area of interest. Its cameras send pictures to a screen on a small handheld unit. A MAV is so light that an operator can catch it on its return like a Frisbee.

Robofly could be considered an extreme example of an MAV. Robofly is a flying robot being developed at the University of California, Berkeley. It is called Robofly because it is a robot aircraft that is actually the size of a fly. One day, squads of roboflies could be sent out to search for targets and collect information about them.

Spy satellites Military satellites orbit the Earth carrying cameras that can see objects on the ground below as small as, perhaps, only 4 cm across. Some of them have infrared cameras that see heat instead of light, so they work in the dark. They also listen to radio communications. Details of spy satellites are top secret, but the latest spy satellites are thought to use stealth technology to make them difficult to find and attack. In future, they may use

lasers instead of radio to send information to Earth. Laser communications are more difficult for an enemy to intercept than radio. When a spacecraft runs out of fuel for its engines, it cannot manoeuvre any more and its working life is over. The latest spy satellites may be capable of being re-fuelled by automatic space tankers, enabling them to stay in space for longer and manoeuvre from place to place more easily.

Electronic warfare Modern warfare relies so heavily on radar, computers, communications and other electronic equipment that a lot of work goes into finding ways to attack enemy electronic systems and protect friendly systems. This is electronic warfare.

How are electronic systems attacked? One way to attack enemy radar and communications is to transmit radio signals that jam them. Electronic warfare aircraft are packed with listening equipment and jamming equipment. As they circle over an area, they pick up enemy radio signals, analyse them and transmit radio signals to jam them. Alternatively, electronic equipment can be knocked out by a new type of weapon called an electronic bomb, or

HOW IT WORKS

The way EMPs work is top secret. They may work by using a high-voltage coil to produce a strong magnetic field. Then an explosive is set off inside the coil. As the explosion moves through the coil, from one end to the other, it compresses the magnetic field ahead of it and strengthens it enormously, sending out a huge electromagnetic pulse, an EMP. When an EMP from an E-bomb hits radio antennae and electronic equipment, it makes large electric currents flow in them, burning out the electronics.

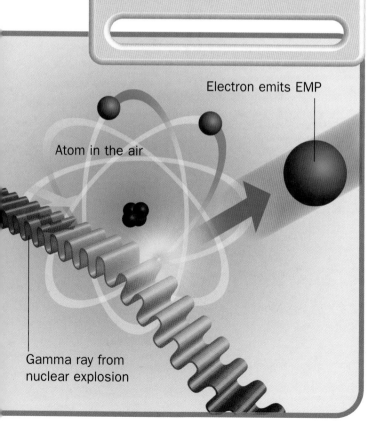

Electron emits EMP

Atom in the air

Gamma ray from nuclear explosion

E-bomb. It produces a powerful burst of energy called an electromagnetic pulse (EMP), which destroys electronic equipment. Any equipment can be protected from EMP by enclosing it in a metal box or cage called a Faraday cage. The simplest Faraday cage could be a cardboard box covered with metal foil. The military version is a custom-built metal container. However, antennae, controls, indicators and sensors have to be outside the cage, so the EMP may still be able to destroy the equipment.

Scientists discovered the effects of electromagnetic pulses when nuclear weapons were being tested in the 1950s, because nuclear explosions produce them. In 1962, a hydrogen bomb test over Johnston Island in the Pacific Ocean produced an EMP powerful enough to blow out 300 street lights 1,600 km away in Hawaii.

Robot spies One alternative to photographing the ground from the air or from space is to put devices on the ground to spy on military activities. These devices are called Unattended Ground Sensors (UGS). There are lots of different types. In addition to

Gamma rays from a nuclear explosion knock electrons out of atoms in the air. These electrons fly away through the Earth's magnetic field and give out a burst of energy called an electromagnetic pulse (EMP).

cameras there are microphones, geophones (vibration detectors), magnetometers, heat sensors and thermal (heat) imagers. The most advanced microphones analyse the sounds they pick up and only raise an alarm when they identify a particular type of sound – from passing tanks for example. The latest sensors can link up with each other and work together. One sensor monitors the nearby area every few seconds, while other nearby sensors stay in a 'sleeping' or standby mode. When it detects something of interest, it 'wakes up' the other sensors to take digital photographs and gather other types of information.

Seabed sensors During the Cold War, the USA wanted to know when Soviet submarines sailed from Russia into the Atlantic Ocean. They put a network of sensors on the seabed near Greenland, Iceland and the UK. It was called SOSUS (SOund SUrveillance System). It picked up the sound of passing submarines. SOSUS is still used today, but only for scientific research.

The aerials on top of these unattended ground sensors send information back to base by radio. Sensors may be camouflaged so they are harder for the enemy to spot. Their batteries keep them working for several weeks or months.

WHAT'S NEXT?

The next generation of ground sensors will be smaller than ever and used in greater numbers than ever. They are called Massively Deployed Unattended Ground Sensors (MDUGS). They are smart enough to communicate with each other and form a map of enemy activity in an area. Two companies are known to be working on MDUGS. There were demonstrations of the systems in 2006. Field tests are going on now and they could be operational by 2011.

CHAPTER 5
non-lethal weapons

Non-lethal weapons are devices that stop enemy troops advancing, or move them out of an area without doing them any serious or lasting harm. They can also be used against rioters and aircraft hijackers.

Non-lethal weapons already in use today include tear gas, water cannons and plastic bullets. The latest non-lethal weapons use dazzling lasers, heat rays, electric shocks and very loud sounds. They are all designed to surprise people or put them out of action in a safe way.

Heat rays Heat rays have been a dream of inventors for centuries. Now there is one that really works. It's called the Active Denial System (ADS). When it is aimed at troops or rioters, it makes them feel as if their skin is burning. It can be mounted on a building that needs protection, but it is also small enough to be carried by a vehicle. This mobile version is called the Vehicle-Mounted Active Denial System (V-MADS). It can be used against people up to about 750 metres away. V-MADS is being developed for

Researchers at the Sandia National Laboratories in New Mexico fine-tune a small-sized Active Denial System (ADS). The small-sized ADS is being developed from the larger military unit. It will be used to protect buildings like nuclear power stations.

HOW IT WORKS

V-MADS works like an amazingly powerful microwave oven. It sends out a narrow beam of microwaves (very short radio waves). When they hit someone, they travel through the skin. They make water molecules in the skin vibrate and heat up. This activates pain sensors in the skin. A two-second burst of the waves can heat skin to 50°C. The pain makes people move away fast, but does no lasting damage.

US military forces. A fully developed system was demonstrated in 2007. It is likely to enter service with US forces in 2010.

Electric shock weapons Electric shock weapons deliver electric shocks to a person's body. The electric shock weapons used today include stun guns and tasers. A stun gun gives

The US Army is testing the Vehicle-Mounted Active Denial System. The antenna on top of the vehicle sends out a beam of energy that people feel as heat.

HOW IT WORKS

The human body controls its muscles by electric signals that travel along nerves from the brain. The body's electrical impulses are tiny, just a fraction of a volt. An electric shock weapon floods the body with between 20,000 and 150,000 volts. It overwhelms the body's own electrical system, which shuts down and muscle control is lost for a while.

someone an electric shock when it is pushed against them and switched on. Tasers fire darts that deliver powerful electric shocks when they hit someone. The electric charge is carried by fine wires that connect the taser to the darts.

More advanced electric shock weapons are being developed. These include electric bullets. They deliver an electric shock to anyone they hit. They can be fired by standard shotguns and grenade launchers. Electric bullets are in the final stage of development.

A taser gun

A taser fires small metal probes at a target up to 6.4 metres away. Hooks anchor the probes in skin or clothing. Then a high-voltage charge travels along wires from the gun to the probes.

WHAT'S NEXT?

The next electric shock weapons will use lasers instead of wires to deliver an electric shock. A laser beam aimed at the target will form a channel through the air that conducts electricity. A fraction of a second later, the high-voltage charge will be sent along this invisible conducting channel, like a lightning flash during a storm. Weapons like this are called electrolasers and are currently in development.

Acoustic weapons Acoustic weapons produce very loud sounds. Troops often use 'flash-bang' charges or flash grenades to surprise enemy forces with a sudden, unexpected explosion. Now, more advanced acoustic weapons are being developed.

The vortex ring gun fires a blank cartridge into a specially shaped barrel that sends out a doughnut-shaped pulse of air. In tests, it was able to knock down a full-size human dummy from 10 metres away. Another weapon called the stick radiator is all electric. It's a tube about a metre long and 4 centimetres across. An electrical

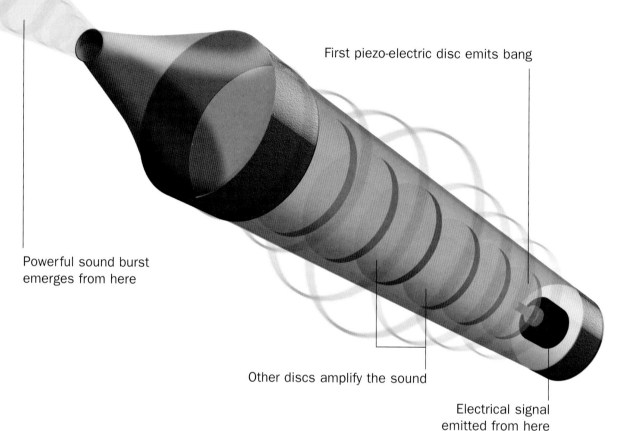

First piezo-electric disc emits bang

Powerful sound burst emerges from here

Other discs amplify the sound

Electrical signal emitted from here

The stick radiator fires bursts of sound created by piezo-electric discs that fire in sequence.

HOW IT WORKS

Acoustic weapons can work in two main ways. First, they can produce sound so loud that it is painful to hear. This makes it very difficult for troops to fight at their best. Second, the 'boom' produced by an acoustic weapon can be so powerful that the shock wave travelling through the air may actually knock someone over.

signal makes a device called a piezo-electric disc send a bang along the tube. This bang is not an explosion but a loud noise and a burst of energy. It reaches a second disc, which produces another bang at exactly the right moment to magnify the first bang. A series of these discs keeps magnifying the sound as it travels down the tube. The result is a painfully loud pulse of sound, that travels through the air like a shock wave, and punches someone like a sound bullet.

Another new weapon called a Pulsed Energy Projectile (PEP) works in a different way. It uses a laser to produce a bright, hot flash. This heats the air so fast, like a bolt of lightning, that it produces a shock wave which travels through the air. It can knock over anyone it hits.

In 2005, pirates attacked a passenger liner off the coast of Somalia. The ship was equipped with LRAD (the Long Range Acoustic Device). LRAD was designed to send out spoken messages over a distance of up to 1,000 metres, like a very loud megaphone, but it can also be used as a weapon. The liner's crew used it to aim loud bangs at the pirates, as if they were under attack. It stopped them from boarding the ship long enough for it to build up speed and out-run the pirate boats.

An operator with a Long Range Acoustic Device (LRAD). An LRAD machine can be used simply to communicate with distant ships as well as deter an actual attack, as happened in Somalia in 2005.

CHAPTER 6
space weapons

Satellites are so important for communications, gathering intelligence, navigation and guiding weapons that they are likely to be attacked in a future war. Weapons may even be stationed in orbit to attack satellites, missiles in flight and targets on the ground.

Satellites under attack Satellites in orbit are in a good position to spot enemy missiles climbing away from their launch pads. They can then sound an early warning of an attack. In a future war, these satellites could be destroyed just before intercontinental missiles are launched. These satellites would probably be attacked with anti-satellite (ASAT) missiles. These missiles have already been developed and tested.

The first anti-satellite missiles were tested in the 1960s. They were not very accurate and they usually missed their targets. There was a suggestion that nuclear weapons might be used instead.

Their blasts would be so powerful that they would not have to actually hit satellites to destroy them. However, they would also have spread deadly radioactive fall-out around the Earth, and if shot down, their nuclear warheads could have landed anywhere. The Outer Space Treaty of 1967 banned the use of nuclear weapons in space. Missiles continued to improve and by the 1980s they had become accurate enough to hit satellites.

This F-15 fighter is carrying an anti-satellite (ASAT) missile underneath it. Flight tests with ASAT missiles began in 1982. They led to the successful destruction of a satellite in space by an air-launched ASAT missile in 1985.

Who has anti-satellite missiles?

The USA and the Soviet Union both tested anti-satellite missiles until the 1980s. They had to end their tests because of the danger to orbiting satellites from wreckage sent flying in all directions by exploding missiles. Some of the debris from these tests still orbits the Earth today. Then on 11 January 2007, China successfully tested an anti-satellite missile by shooting down one of its own old weather satellites.

An anti-satellite (ASAT) missile soars away from an F-15 fighter. The aircraft pulls up into a steep climb before firing the missile. The missile then climbs into space and homes in on its target.

FOR AND AGAINST

For
- Weapons in space could attack targets anywhere on Earth without having to fly through other countries' air-spaces.
- They could also attack satellites in space.

Against
- They would spark a new arms race in space.
- Exploding weapons and satellites in space would spread dangerous debris around the Earth.

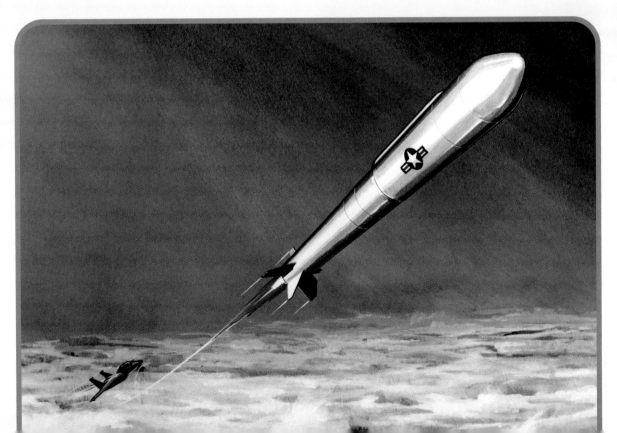

Anti-satellite satellites Anti-satellite satellites could be used to attack enemy satellites instead of missiles. They work by manoeuvring close to an enemy satellite and exploding. Another way to knock out satellites without blowing them up is to blind their cameras by firing lasers at them from the ground or from an aircraft. This has the advantage of putting satellites out of action without producing any debris or wreckage in space.

Other space weapons One space weapon being researched now does not use any explosives or lasers. It is a satellite armed with large tungsten rods. Each of the metal rods is about 6 metres long and 30 centimetres across. They would be fired at a target on Earth, hitting it without warning at more than 13,000 kph. The speed and weight of the rod would make it amazingly destructive. It could penetrate buildings, tanks and even underground bunkers.

'STAR WARS'

Star Wars is the nickname of a US project called the Strategic Defense Initiative (SDI) in the 1980s. It was to use weapons on the ground and in space to protect the USA from missile attacks. The system was to include laser weapons in space, but they proved to be impractical. However the different parts of the SDI system – such as missiles, lasers and railguns, weapons in space and sensors – are still being developed.

A Titan 1 missile is destroyed by a laser in a test at the White Sands Missile Range in New Mexico. The experiment was carried out to test the effectiveness of laser weapons as part of the Star Wars project.

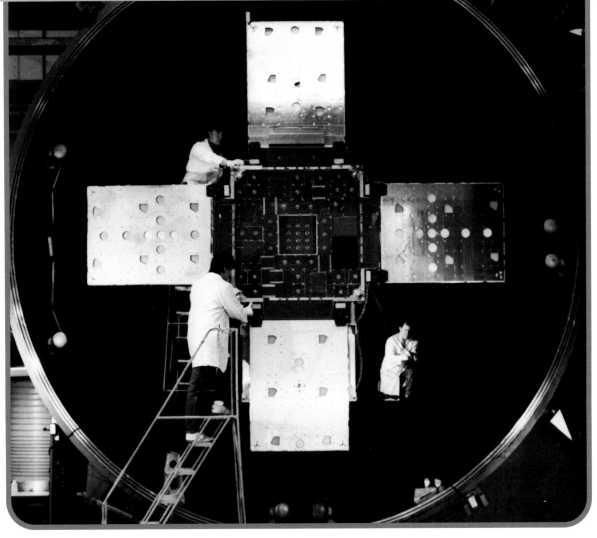

Technicians work on the Low-power Atmospheric Compensation Experiment (LACE) satellite. This satellite was an important part of developing laser weapons for the Strategic Defense Initiative (SDI), or Star Wars, project.

Will there be manned military spacecraft? There are manned military vehicles on land and water, underwater and in the air. In future, there will very likely be manned military spacecraft, too. There have already been military space stations. Three of Russia's seven *Salyut* space stations in the 1970s were military. They were mainly used for photo-reconnaissance, taking highly detailed photographs of certain parts of the Earth. One of them, *Salyut 3*, was even armed with a gun. After its crew left, the gun was successfully test-fired in space. The US *Space Shuttle* has carried out military space missions, too. In future, there are likely to be more manned military spacecraft flown by military astronauts.

conclusion

Military powers used to compete with each other to arm themselves with the most powerful weapons. Now, countries are concentrating their efforts on developing smaller, smarter weapons.

Trends in technology In the twentieth century, the trend towards more and more powerful weapons and longer range weapons led to the most powerful and longest-range weapons ever created – intercontinental nuclear missiles. In the twenty-first century, military technology is trying to do more with less. Military technology is also more accurate than ever. Greater accuracy means that fewer weapons can be used, causing fewer casualties.

The information war We live in the information age. Information has never been more important in warfare too. The challenge for the future is to develop ways of bringing all the data, pictures, maps and other information together, analysing it quickly and presenting it to troops on the ground in a way that they can take in fast and use before it is out of date. Future soldiers may have important information projected onto the inside of their helmet visor.

Modern military operations require the collection and analysis of enormous amounts of information. This is often managed from at least one control room. This room is the System Control Room for the Iraq war, which began in 2003, at Camp Doha in Qatar.

Robots The numbers of military robots are set to increase rapidly. The USA is aiming to replace one third of its armed vehicles and weaponry with robots by 2015.

How does military technology affect us? We all make use of military technology in one way or another. The Internet was developed as a way of protecting computer systems from a military attack. The technology used for weather forecasts can trace its history back to photo-reconnaissance in both world wars. The rockets that launch satellites and spacecraft were developed from rocket-powered weapons built in the 1940s. GPS satellite navigation used by drivers was developed for military use.

Fighting terrorism The 9/11 attacks on the USA in 2001 showed that terrorist organisations can bypass the most high-tech military weapons and forces to attack cities. Much of the military technology developed up to now is useless against terrorist attack. Future military technology will have to find new ways of fighting terrorism. However, many of these techniques will violate the privacy of millions of people, who will have to decide how much privacy they are prepared to give up for increased security.

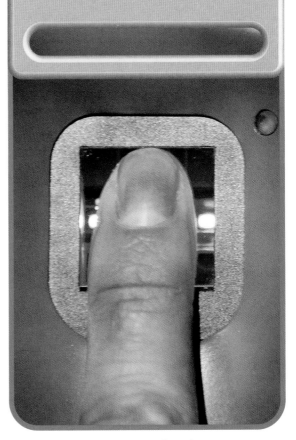

WHAT'S NEXT?

Information technology is the weapon that will be used against terrorists. Facial recognition systems will identify known terrorists on city streets. Computerised cameras will spot unusual body language that may reveal a terrorist. Automatic analysis of electronic communication will give early warning of attacks being planned. Electronic sniffers will detect explosives and other dangerous chemicals.

New security systems, such as biometric fingerprint scanning, are already being introduced at airports around the world.

glossary

acoustic To do with sound. An acoustic weapon is a weapon that uses sound.

antennae The parts of radio systems that send out or receive radio signals.

artificial intelligence The development of computers which can reason in a similar way to the human brain.

autonomous Independent. An autonomous aircraft flies under its own control without a pilot.

classified Information that should only be seen by certain authorised personnel.

Cold War The period of hostility between democratic and communist countries after World War II.

exoskeleton Literally, an 'external skeleton'. A powered robot-like suit or frame that enables a soldier to carry a heavier load or move faster.

gamma ray High-energy electromagnetic radiation.

gunship A helicopter or aeroplane heavily armed with guns.

hull The part of a ship that sits in the water.

hypersonic Faster than Mach 5 (five times the speed of sound).

infrared Invisible lightwaves whose wavelength is longer than light but shorter than radio waves.

intercontinental missile A missile that can travel from one continent to another.

laser A device that produces an intensely powerful beam of light. Laser stands for Light Amplification by Stimulated Emission of Radiation.

microwaves Very short radio waves, 1-30 millimetres long.

payload The passengers, cargo or bombs carried by an aircraft.

prototype The first full-size, working version of something. Prototypes are built to test vehicles and weapons before they are manufactured in large numbers.

radar A system for detecting and locating aircraft, rockets, ships and other vehicles and weapons by sending out radio waves and picking up any reflections that bounce back after striking these objects. Radar stands for Radio Detection And Ranging.

reconnaissance Spying on enemy forces or land. Aircraft and satellites are often used for reconnaissance by flying over an area and photographing it. This is also called photo-reconnaissance.

stealth plane A military aircraft designed to be hard to find by radar.

submersible A small underwater vehicle.

supersonic Something that travels faster than the speed of sound.

further information

Books

Dilemmas in Modern Science: Technology by Jon Turney, Evans Brothers Ltd, 2008.

The World's Greatest Warplanes by Ian Graham, Raintree Publishers, 2005.

Technology All Around Us: Aircraft, by Kay Woodward and Andrew Woodward, Smart Apple Media, 2005.

Websites

Find out more about future soldiers and their equipment at:
http://en.wikipedia.org/wiki/ Future_Force_Warrior

See how military robots works at:
http://science.howstuffworks.com/ military-robot.htm

Read 50 fascinating facts about US nuclear weapons at:
www.brook.edu/fp/projects/nucwcost/ 50.htm

Learn more about an Abrams tank at:
http://military.discovery.com/convergence/abr ams/explore/explore.html

Find out how military satellite navigation works at:
www.nasm.si.edu/gps/work.html

You can read about the Littoral Combat Ship, the US Navy's new trimaran warship at:
http://www.defense-update.com/products/ l/lcs-independence.htm

Are supersonic submarines possible? Find out at:
http://www.space.com/businesstechnology/ technology/gear_supercavitation.html

Places to visit

Imperial War Museum, London
Displays of military technology and events from World War I to the present day (www.iwm.org.uk).

Imperial War Museum Duxford, Duxford, Cambridgeshire
Europe's premier aviation museum (http://duxford.iwm.org.uk).

Fleet Air Arm Museum, RNAS Yeovilton, Near Ilchester, Somerset
Europe's biggest naval aviation museum (http://www.fleetairarm.com).

The Helicopter Museum, Locking Moor Road, Weston-super-Mare, Somerset
The world's biggest helicopter collection (http://www.helicoptermuseum.co.uk).

The Royal Navy Submarine Museum, Gosport, Hampshire, England
The official Royal Navy submarine museum and home of the Royal Navy's first operational submarine, the 1901 Holland 1 (www.rnsubmus.co.uk).

index